Recognize and ward off dark psychology

How to recognize emotional manipulation, expose a personality disorder and lies and skillfully fend off manipulation techniques

Martina Richter

CONTENTS

What you can expect in this guide

Do you feel manipulated and deceived? Do you trust people too easily and allow yourself to be blinded by them? Do you have the feeling that you always end up with the wrong people and end up being surprised by their cold-heartedness? Or have you caught a manipulator and want to understand their behavior? Then you have made the right decision by buying this guide.

A dark side lurks in many people. They use psychological tricks to manipulate those around them and play them off against each other. They use people cold-heartedly to achieve their own goals and rarely feel remorse or regret. Have you also had experiences with cold-hearted people and want to understand their behavior? This guide will give you answers to all your questions about dark psychology. You will learn all about the dark side of psychology. What constitutes it and how to recognize people with a dark side.

You will get to know the dark triad of personality and understand it using examples. Because only when you have understood what makes a person with a dark side so dangerous will you know why you should avoid them if possible. However, you will not always recognize a dark personality immediately. They usually only show their true colors years later. That's why this guide will help you to recognize the signs that a person with dark characteristics is operating in your immediate environment. You will gain an insight into deception and manipulation techniques and also learn how to uncover lies and influence by others. In the final chapter of the guide, you will learn how to use psychological tricks to negotiate successfully and persuade others.

Understanding the dark side

WHAT IS THE DARK SIDE?

Before you can learn how to put these strategies into practice, you must first understand what the dark side of psychology is all about. You need to understand which characteristics are attributed to the dark side in order to recognize them. Both socially and morally questionable behavior is usually attributed to dark personality traits. People with more pronounced dark personality traits are usually characterized by manipulative, selfish, self-serving or callous behaviour. However, not all characteristics of the dark side are usually equally pronounced. What they usually all have in common, however, is a lack of empathy and understanding as well as a pronounced lack of emotion. Although many of the dark traits have negative connotations, they are often associated with professional success.

In recent years, scientists have developed psychological tests that can be used to determine dark personality traits. Nevertheless, it is difficult to obtain a valid test result, especially in the case of manipulative people. Observations and conversations are therefore just as important in uncovering a person's dark side.

HOW IS IT CREATED?

You now have a rough overview of the characteristics and behavior that make up the dark side of the personality. But how does it develop? Have people with dark personality traits experienced a lot of suffering themselves or have these traits been inherited?

There is not just one answer to these questions, as there are several factors responsible for us developing a dark side. I will now tell you exactly what these are.

In order to understand why a person has dark personality traits, researchers and scientists in the field of psychology have long been studying the conditions under which certain personality characteristics develop. What should be clear to everyone is that there is no single experience that causes every person to develop a dark personality. Rather, it is an interplay of genetic, biological and environmental factors that leads to the development of dark personality traits. One model that explains the development of a dark personality through to a personality disorder is the vulnerability-stress model. The model assumes that some people are biologically more vulnerable to developing a mental disorder than others. Genetically inherited personality traits, such as strong impulsivity or sensitivity, can make a person more vulnerable or susceptible to developing a mental disorder. In childhood and adolescence, stressful conditions, such as negative parenting styles or the death of a parent, can further promote the development of a mental illness. If a person also has few positive experiences, few trusted caregivers and is otherwise exposed to less positive environmental conditions, a mental disorder can manifest itself.

The development of certain personality traits and possibly personality disorders is thought to be influenced by genetic components that increase the likelihood of developing certain personality traits. Scientific studies have shown that identical twins have more similar personality traits than fraternal twins. This means that genetic factors influence the development of personality. If fraternal twins were just as similar in terms of personality traits, this would be primarily due to environmental conditions. Nevertheless, it cannot be assumed that a dark personality exists across generations. Not every person with a genetic component for dark personality traits will develop them. Here again, the vulnerability-stress model must be taken into account.

In addition to the genetic component, environmental influences also have an impact on the development of personality traits. Researchers state that experiences of separation and loss, neglect and abuse in childhood and adolescence can lead to a person developing a dark personality. For example, long-term exposure to abuse or a negative parenting style can have a lasting effect on how a person deals with their own feelings, how they deal with the feelings of others and how they form relationships with other people.

Particularly in people who exhibit narcissistic traits, such as having to constantly place themselves at the center of attention, a lack of emotional warmth, inadequate boundary setting and the link between success and recognition may have led to the manifestation of these personality traits in childhood. They only received praise, warmth and love when they had achieved something particularly great, and accordingly also present themselves as particularly great or special in adulthood in order to receive recognition. Nevertheless, it must be noted that the development of each person's personality is influenced by their own experiences. Each person has an individual genetic make-up and resilience, which can lead to a person developing a dark personality or depression when experiencing a stressful situation or remaining mentally healthy.

Scientists and researchers assume that personality development is not largely complete until the age of 16. The diagnosis of personality disorder, which you will learn about later in this guide, is therefore not given before the age of 16.

The dark core of the personality

The dark core of the personality is generally reflected in a person's behavior. The dark core consists of the tendency to maximize one's own benefit without any consideration for the feelings and needs of other people. They take advantage of themselves at the expense of others. They see themselves as particularly important and superior. However, this does not mean that people with a dark core cannot cooperate well with others. In order to avoid sanctions or protect their reputation, they are usually excellent at working with others.

Of course, the dark core of the personality is not equally pronounced in all people. Certain dark personality traits, such as manipulation, lying or callousness, are also more pronounced in one person than another. Nevertheless, dark personality traits are inter-related. This means that if you meet a person who is very manipulative, it is more likely that this person will also lie frequently. The three dark personality traits are also related to each other. These are narcissism, Machiavellianism and psychopathy, also known as the dark triad of personality. You will now get to know these three traits in more detail and also learn how to identify them in people.

You may have already come across the term "dark triad". These are three well-researched personality traits that have the common goal of achieving their own goals and personal success at the expense of others.

Narcissism: Describes the characteristic of judging oneself as more valuable, more important, better and greater than one actually is. Narcissists have an exaggerated sense of self-importance, are very self-centered and stand out due to their exaggerated positive self-assessment. They have little regard for other people's feelings and are quick to hurt others emotionally.

They are satisfied with themselves and their lives, but want to be admired by others at all times. At first glance, a narcissist can even appear likeable, as they are usually very charismatic and charming. They are very eloquent and magically attract attention. However, over time it becomes clear that he is only doing all this for himself and needs the attention and admiration for his ego.

A narcissist can tolerate derogatory remarks just as little internally as criticism. Outwardly, however, they appear immune to any kind of criticism. Although many of these traits are considered negative, they can also have a positive effect to a healthy degree and help you get ahead in your job.

Machiavellianism: Includes the traits of striving for power, greatness and influence. Machiavellians are cynical, egotistical and manipulative. They will use any means to achieve their own goals. They develop strategies and tactical approaches to gain power and influence. As they are able to show empathy, they quickly gain the trust of other people and build up a network from which they can only benefit. They accept hurting others through their actions and usually only enter into friendships and relationships if they are of benefit to them.

They often take advantage of their fellow human beings and manipulate them. Their skillful self-presentation makes it easy for them to make contacts and win people over. Like a chameleon, Machiavellians are able to adapt flexibly to new situations and camouflage their bad character traits. It is therefore often difficult to unmask them.

Psychopathy: This is probably the darkest of the three characteristics. Psychopaths are unscrupulous, selfish and manipulative liars. They feel no remorse and are very callous. They usually lack the ability to empathize, so they take advantage of people and have no regard for the emotional consequences of their actions. They have no moral conscience.

With their charming nature, they maintain superficial relationships that serve to achieve their own goals. However, they usually lack long-term, realistic goals and use the exploitation and manipulation of people to combat boredom. Psychopaths are often criminals and can be found in prisons. Even in adolescence, psychopathy is associated with delinquent and criminal behavior. In contrast, "successful psychopaths" are usually found in leadership positions.

HOW DO YOU RECOGNIZE DARK PERSONALITIES?

Now you know what constitutes a dark personality and which traits belong to the dark triad of personality. People with these traits are often difficult to deal with over a long period of time, and you often wish you had recognized the signs afterwards.

Therefore, you will now learn how to recognize a dark personality and how to expose its benefit-oriented behaviour. You must learn to listen and observe carefully in order to recognize possible signs and read between the lines.

1. A person **often changes relationships and friendships** because they quickly become bored, have already exploited or manipulated them.

2. **superficial relationships**. She finds it difficult to have deep relationships. She prefers to have many and changing contacts.

3. **the charming gentleman**. They maintain relationships through their charming manner.

4. **changing sexual partners**. After the conquest they are bored and want to move on.

5 A person **does not apologize**. They feel no remorse and cannot recognize mistakes.

6. **retain control**. She must make the decisions.

7. **little empathy**. The person has little ability to empathize with others.

8. **ambition**.

9. **exaggerated self-esteem**. The person thinks they are special and has an exaggerated sense of self-importance.

10. **lies**.

One well-known film character who, according to Australian psychologist Peter Jonason, is a prime example of a dark personality is Bond. James Bond. Because, although he makes countless women's hearts beat faster, his enemies come first for him. With no regard for the feelings of those around him, Bond will do anything to achieve his goals. He is only interested in his own advantage and will literally walk over dead bodies to achieve it. Nevertheless, he is charming, charismatic and polite. He knows how to behave and how to win women's hearts with skill. He has a dangerous combination of manipulation, unscrupulousness and stubbornness that can be classified as part of the dark triad.

Bond's narcissism: expensive cars and suits, attracts attention, eloquent.

Bond's Machiavellianism: tactical approach, strong target-oriented focus, flexibly adaptable to new situations.

Bond's psychopathy: His "license to kill" represents the ruthless way he gets rid of people who hinder him in achieving his goal.

However, such a clear classification and pure form of the dark triad usually only exists in Hollywood films. In reality, it is very rare. It is therefore important to pay attention to the signs, but not to jump to conclusions.

HOW DO YOU DEAL WITH DARK PERSONALITIES?

If you now know a person who has many of these characteristics or has perhaps even exploited you unscrupulously and cold-heartedly, how should you deal with them? In the following chapter, you will learn what you should bear in mind when dealing with people with a dark personality.

Narcissism:

1. **Gentle handling**: People with narcissistic personality traits are very sensitive. Criticism must therefore be expressed cautiously and carefully. Try to formulate your criticism in the form of precise "I" messages. "I suffer when you don't keep appointments".

2. **Do not expect apologies**. A person with narcissistic traits cannot admit to themselves that they have made a mistake. This does not fit in with their grandiose self-image.

3. **Ask, don't demand**: You should not expect a narcissistic person to respond to your request. Nevertheless, requests are usually more successful than

demands.

4. **Keep the focus**: Narcissists are usually good at distracting from the issue and try to prioritize their own goals and needs. Keep your focus and don't allow yourself to be distracted from your goals.

5. **Strengthen your communication skills**: Be aware of what you want to achieve with your communication. Language is power.

6. **Present objective facts**: The narcissist often tries to push himself into a "victim role". Use objective facts to make it clear to them why this is not the case.

7. **Protect your own boundaries**: There are no rules or boundaries for a narcissist. He believes that he is above everything. You should therefore not respond to anything that goes beyond your own boundaries and moral standards.

8. **Keep your distance**: If everything becomes too much for you, keep your distance. You can't change a narcissist.

9. **Feed the ego**: If you have no way of avoiding the narcissist or keeping your distance in a certain situation, it helps to feed your ego with compliments. Although this can be difficult, it is better than becoming the target of narcissistic aggression.

10. **Realize that the problem is not with you**: People with narcissistic traits will not communicate with you as equals because they think they are something special and better.

Machiavellianism:

1. **Check statements for their truthfulness**: The Machiavellian is very determined and manipulative. Protect yourself by checking the truthfulness of his statements.

2. **Question his intentions**: A Machiavellian person will tell you everything you want to hear in order to achieve your own goals. You should therefore ask y-ourself what the intention behind his behavior is.

3. **don't let yourself be blinded**: Because unlike psychopaths and narcissists, you can come across as very empathetic.

4. **do not give in**: Machiavellians are strong negotiators. Make your stance and position clear to him. However, do not annoy him.

5 **Remain friendly and firm**: Don't make yourself a target by reacting defiantly in conversations. By communicating in a friendly and assertive manner, you convey to him that you are communicating on the same level.

6. **repartee**: Defending yourself against the Machiavellian's manipulation with repartee aims to create distance and give you a few seconds to think and still say "no".

7. **protect your own boundaries**: Even for a Machiavellian, there are no rules or boundaries. He believes that he is above everything. You should therefore not respond to anything that exceeds your own boundaries and moral standards.

8. **keep your distance**: Here too, if everything becomes too much for you, keep your distance. You can't change a Machiavellian.

9. **Feeding the ego**: If you have no way of avoiding the Machiavellian or keeping your distance in a certain situation, it also helps to feed your ego with compliments.

10. **Realize that the problem is not with you**: People with Machiavellian traits will not communicate with you as equals.

Psychopathy:

1. **Trust your gut feeling**: If the other person seems threatening, trust them and keep your distance.

2. **Self-confident gestures and facial expressions**: Psychopaths rarely manipulate people with a self-confident demeanor.

3. **Don't show weakness**: A psychopath focuses on the weaknesses of others in order to exploit them.

4. **be careful**: never put yourself on the same level as a psychopath. He is a professional at what he does.

5 **Protect your own boundaries**: Even for a psychopath, there are no rules or boundaries. You should therefore not respond to anything that exceeds your own boundaries and moral standards.

6 **React calmly**: The psychopath gets bored quickly and may let you go and look for something else to do.

7. **don't stay alone**: tell friends or other people about the problem. Together it is easier to take action against a psychopath.

8. **keep your distance**: Again, keep your distance. You can't change a psychopath.

9. **report**: Do not hesitate to report the acts of the psychopath in case of serious offenses. The psychopath is ruthless. It is highly likely to happen again.

10**. realize that the problem is not with you**: People with psychopathic traits will not communicate with you on an equal footing .

Do not hesitate to get help. You never know how far a person with dark personality traits would go to achieve their goals. However, the majority of people only have dark personality traits. A pure form of dark personality is very rare.

DARK PERSONALITIES IN THE WORK ENVIRONMENT

In your working environment, you are bound to come across people with a dark personality. The best thing to do in such a situation would certainly be to keep your distance and avoid the person. However, especially in the office and when working in a team, this is usually not a feasible solution. People with Machiavellian personality traits are particularly common at management level. They are seen as competitive and assertive.

At first glance, this can bring many advantages for a company. But if you take a closer look, it quickly becomes clear that employees suffer under such leadership. The management skills of a manager with

Machiavellian traits are usually judged to be inadequate and employees are put off by his manipulative behavior.

People with narcissistic personality traits are also convincing at first glance, especially in job interviews. It is only over time that the true character of a narcissistic colleague or boss is revealed. They display their egotistical, manipulative behavior and employees who work with them are usually quickly exhausted and burnt out. To prevent power struggles with them, it is best to clarify areas of responsibility in advance and set clear boundaries. As they are particularly easily offended and tend to seek revenge in this context, care should be taken to avoid accusations and threats.

Psychopaths can also be encountered in the workplace. Working together usually begins quite normally, but the true face is revealed as things progress. Values, morals and agreements do not exist for him. They are cold, calculating and heartless. It is noticeable that the higher the hierarchical level, the more frequently the leaders exhibit psychopathic traits. Various studies speak of up to 20 %. It usually takes a long time before a psychopath is exposed in the work environment and ultimately has to leave the company. Here too, it is helpful to confide in a trusted colleague or even the HR department. Don't let him isolate you and act consistently.

10 general tips to keep in mind if you encounter a person with dark personality traits in your work environment:

1. document critical incidents precisely.

2. confide in a caregiver.

3. do not allow yourself to be isolated.

4. show boundaries.

5. be aware of your own strengths.

6. do not get involved in games.

7. take a break for unpleasant topics.

8. show self-confidence.

9. stay on the factual level.

10. try to keep your distance and keep your distance.

DARK PERSONALITIES IN THE PARTNERSHIP

Although people with dark personality traits find it particularly difficult to enter into relationships, narcissists in particular long for love and recognition. But is a dark personality even capable of loving someone else? And how should you deal with a partner who exhibits personality traits from the dark triad? Can a relationship work at all?

Psychotherapist Claas-Hinrich Lammers gives a clear answer to the latter question: "It depends entirely on your own capacity for suffering. A relationship with a narcissist, Machiavellian or psychopath can be exhausting and exhausting. Many people don't even realize that they are entering into a relationship with a person with dark personality traits. Love is known to be blind. But if you notice these signs, you should take a closer look behind your partner's façade:

1. he/she is obsessed with winning. Everything is a competition.

2. he/she has a low frustration tolerance.

3. he/she has secrets.

4. he/she wants to have the power.

5. he/she is lying.

6. because of you/because of me, others neglect social contacts.

7. he/she is very charming.

8. he/she has no morals.

9. he/she knows no boundaries.

10. he/she often threatens to end the relationship.

A narcissist as a partner

As narcissists like to be the center of attention and need a lot of attention, they tend to look for a partner who is less self-confident and more insecure in life.

As a partner, you must submit to your narcissistic partner. In the relationship, you will endure many humiliations and fits of anger. He will demand a lot of understanding from you, but will show you none himself. You should banish the thought of being able to change your narcissistic partner from your mind, because it won't happen. A narcissist cannot be changed.

Nevertheless, a relationship with a narcissist can also have its advantages: It will never be boring, you will meet lots of new people, he is a good protector and gives great gifts to make himself the center of attention. However, due to the massive difficulties in dealing with narcissistic people, a partnership is usually characterized by problems that ultimately lead to separation. Breaking up with a narcissistic partner is usually particularly difficult, as they perceive "being left" as a personal criticism of themselves. A break-up gnaws at their dignity and self-esteem for years to come. He will try to prevent a separation by any means necessary. An emotional dependency that has built up over the years becomes particularly clear now. You must remain strong and not allow yourself to be drawn in by him.

A Machiavellian as a partner

Machiavellians are particularly good at disguising themselves, so it can be years before you expose your partner. They place themselves above their partner and manipulate them. The Machiavellian's true face is gradually revealed through immoral, self-serving behavior.

As he is very power-hungry, it can also happen that he strongly controls his partner. A relationship with them consists of many lows, but also highs. His partner is usually trapped in a vicious circle of love and suffering. It can therefore take a long time before you finally make the decision to separate from your partner with Machiavellian traits. Especially strong women with a strong sense of self-worth will want to separate from him. When separating from him, you should make sure to break emotional dependencies and question the intentions of his behavior. They also usually want to remain friends with their ex-partner for practical reasons.

A psychopath as a partner

Psychopaths are often difficult to see through at the beginning of a relationship. They are true masters at spoiling their partner with gifts and also sexually. Conquering a woman is a fascinating and exciting game for him. However, once he has conquered her, his behavior usually changes quickly. He wants to feel superior and starts to hide things.

He doesn't want to be responsible for anything, wants to control you and quickly becomes aggressive and abusive. Your alarm bells should be ringing at this point at the latest. If you want to separate from your partner with psychopathic traits, there are a few things you should bear in mind. He will feel neither guilt nor remorse for the actions you accuse him of. He won't apologize for anything either. In his mind, you are his property to use as he pleases. He sees himself as a person who leaves others and is not abandoned by his partner. He will do anything to keep you with him. This can even lead to threats. He will try to put you in a bad light so as not to look like a loser himself. If possible, confide in someone you know or get professional help. A psychopath is cunning and will leave no stone unturned to keep you with them. Stay strong and be aware that he has no empathy or morals and can therefore be very dangerous.

Karin, 51, talked about her relationship with a psychopath in an interview with a magazine:

"After two months, he asked me to marry him." I was the woman of his life. In the months that followed, I ignored a lot of things, I know that today. If I had been in my right mind, I should have been suspicious that I wasn't even allowed to look at other men. Then he feared for our great love, as he explained to me, complaining . *He himself was flirting like hell* with the waitress in the restaurant. When I approached him about it, he said it was total nonsense, that I was looking at it all wrong. I should also have been suspicious that he was ripping me off like a Christmas goose. *I was allowed to pay for everything,* even though we both earned the same amount, he as an insurance salesman, me as a media consultant. He just didn't have any

money with him in the restaurant and he was never embarrassed. And I should have noticed that he was driving my friends away, one by one." In an interview with "Idee für mich".
Available at: https://www.idee-fuer-mich.de/leben/aus-dem-leben/verliebt-in-einen-psychopathen-4050.html.

FAMOUS PEOPLE WITH DARK PERSONALITY TRAITS

Many successful and creative personalities are said to have dark personality traits. You may have heard rumors and accusations yourself. This chapter introduces you to personalities who are said to have dark personality traits.

However, these quotes are not related to a diagnosed personality disorder and only serve to illustrate the disorder. Try to guess from the stories which dark trait the person embodies.

"Imagine this boss: He has a perverse desire to belittle others. His tantrums are legendary. Statements like "You asshole, you do everything wrong" occur hourly. He completely lacks empathy. He wraps people up with charm when it's convenient for him. He ignores reality and claims to be someone special. Morality doesn't count. He unscrupulously cheats on his best friend. At the same time, he is highly charismatic. According to an Insead study, this man is the most successful manager of all time: Steve Jobs." (Johannes Steyrer, derstandard.at, 07.06.2014).   Psychopathy

"In the case of the president, it is quite obvious that his psychological need is to appear invulnerable like Superman. In order to maintain such a grandiose facade, someone with such a weak ego is even willing to sacrifice the lives of others. Every waking moment of his life he asks himself, how can I make people admire me? Because otherwise I can't breathe. That's how obsessed he is with it. It's hard to have to live your life like that." (Dr. Ramani Durvasula on Trump, deutschlandfunk.de, 14.10.2020).   Narcissism

"The fascination with the strong, charismatic ruler has never faded. He convinces his people that he can perform miracles, that he represents the nation. They do that [...] skillfully. By adopting a virtual superego, they appear to be more than they actually are. They are saviors and problem solvers - that goes down well in our increasingly complex world. And if you are blessed with this charisma, you are no longer accountable to anyone. [...] Machiavellianism suggests potency, defensiveness. The macho aspect is part of the powerful self-portrayal, such as the pictures [...] [of the one] with a naked upper body. All of this is intended to convey the message of power and strength." (Gudrun Dometeit, on Putin and Erdoğan, Fokus Magazin online, Politics and Society, 26.03.2017). Machiavellianism

Personality disorders

Many people exhibit personality traits of the dark triad. However, only a few have a pronounced personality disorder. But what is a personality disorder and how many people have a dark personality disorder? You will find answers to these questions in this chapter.

A personality disorder is a mental disorder that is associated with an altered personality structure. People with a personality disorder exhibit inappropriate behavior in relationships and everyday situations. This persists over time and across different situations. Over time, this causes the person affected to suffer.

Personality disorders are rarely diagnosed before the age of 16, as a person's personality is still developing up to this age. Personality disorders that are associated with characteristics of the dark triad are narcissistic personality disorder and dissocial personality disorder.

Frequency and gender distribution

In Germany, around 8% of adults suffer from a personality disorder. Women are affected just as often as men. One exception is dissocial personality disorder. Men are affected by this disorder up to three times more often than women. Dissocial personality disorder occurs in around 3% of German men and 1% of German women. If we look at narcissistic personality disorder, up to 2.5% of German men and women suffer from this personality disorder. As both disorders are relatively rare in the population, psychologists and psychiatrists often use the term personality accentuation when the full clinical picture of the disorder is not present.

WHAT IS NARCISSISTIC PERSONALITY DISORDER?

In the case of narcissistic personality disorder, those affected exhibit the characteristics of narcissism of the dark triad. They have little empathy, overestimate their own abilities and strive for attention and recognition. They exaggerate, lie, deceive, manipulate and react more intensely than other people to criticism and rejection.

In the case of narcissistic personality disorder, however, the characteristics are so pronounced that the person affected suffers from them themselves. They are unable to adapt well to external life circumstances. Their pronounced desire for recognition and admiration usually stands in their way. Narcissistic personality disorder is therefore present when a person has very pronounced narcissistic personality traits and suffers from them. However, narcissists do not always reveal their character traits. In addition to overt narcissists, who reveal their grandiosity and avoidable superiority, there are also covert narcissists. They are friendly, generous and helpful. But this only serves to put themselves in the right light through their altruistic actions.

Narcissism can also be characterized by vulnerability and closed-mindedness. In contrast to grandiose narcissists, who reveal their exaggerated ego, it is difficult to diagnose covert, vulnerable narcissists. Narcissistic personality disorder is usually accompanied by other psychological disorders such as eating disorders, depression and drug abuse. A narcissistic personality disorder is a serious illness and can have serious consequences if not treated properly.

HOW DO YOU RECOGNIZE A NARCISSISTIC PERSONALITY DISORDER?

In Germany, narcissistic personality disorder is diagnosed according to the International Classification of Mental Disorders (ICD-10). The book contains criteria, a certain number of which must be fulfilled in order to be able to make a diagnosis of narcissistic personality disorder.

The diagnosis requires several intensive discussions and psychological tests may also be used. As a layperson, you should therefore not use the criteria to freely distribute the diagnosis and label others. Nevertheless, you can use the criteria to assess whether an appointment with a psychologist, psychiatrist or psychotherapist should be considered.

The following criteria are proposed for diagnosis (ICD-10, p. 349):

1. **sense of grandeur in relation to one's own importance** (e.g. exaggerating one's own performance).
2. **preoccupation with fantasies of unlimited success, power, splendor, beauty or ideal love**.
3. **he/she is convinced that he/she is special or unique**. Only people who are also special can be with him/her or understand him/her.
4. **need for excessive admiration.**
5. **unreasonable expectation of special or preferential treatment from others**.
6. **taking advantage of other people to achieve your own goals**.
7. **lack of empathy**.
8. **envy.**
9. **arrogant, haughty behavior**.

In general, the behavior must persist across situations and should not be socially or culturally acceptable.

WHAT IS DISSOCIAL PERSONA-
LITY DISORDER?

After learning about narcissistic personality disorder, you will now also become acquainted with dissocial personality disorder. Dissocial personality disorder is also known as antisocial personality disorder. As the name suggests, the behavior of affected individuals is characterized by irresponsibility and manipulation.

The focus is on disregarding and violating the basic rights of others. Like psychopaths, people with a dissocial personality disorder show no remorse. They act very impulsively, which makes them dangerous and inscrutable. They are also quick to display aggressive behavior. They destroy other people's property, steal or mistreat animals or people. They cheat and deceive, and may also try to conceal their actions under an alias. People with a dissocial personality disorder are masters at manipulating and lying. They usually only do this for their own pleasure or to achieve their own goals. Dissocial behavior such as torturing animals, bullying at school or stealing things can already be observed in childhood and adolescence before the diagnosis is made. It is also striking that the proportion of people with a dissocial personality disorder in prisons is significantly higher than in the general population. Nevertheless, this does not mean that every person with a dissocial personality disorder automatically becomes delinquent and criminal.

A dissocial personality disorder is often accompanied by increased substance use such as alcohol or depression as well as psychopathy. In contrast to psychopaths, people with a dissocial personality disorder are not as good at disguising their behavior. People with a dissocial personality disorder usually do not exhibit the initially charming, approachable nature of psychopaths. Nevertheless, there are many overlaps between the two disorders.

HOW DO YOU RECOGNIZE A DIS-SOCIAL PERSONALITY DISOR-DER?

Like narcissistic personality disorder, dissocial or anti-social personality disorder is diagnosed in Germany according to the International Classification of Mental Disorders (ICD-10). Here too, a precise diagnosis requires several intensive interviews and psychological tests.

You should never make the assumption that a person has a dissocial personality disorder lightly. The ICD-10 criteria can provide an indication of the possible presence of this disorder. However, the diagnosis should only be made by trained professionals.

The following criteria are proposed for diagnosis (ICD-10, p. 239f.):

1. emotional coldness.
2. persistent, irresponsible attitude, disregard for standards.
3. no lasting relationships.
4. very low frustration tolerance.
5. no sense of guilt.

6. blaming others for your own misconduct.

IS A PERSONALITY DISORDER TREATABLE?

Yes, a personality disorder is generally treatable with psychotherapeutic support. Nevertheless, the first hurdle of seeking help must first be overcome. Those affected often find it difficult to seek or accept help. As a personality disorder is an ego-syntonic disorder, those affected usually do not even realize that their behaviour is inappropriate. Ego-syntonic means that those affected perceive their impulses and feelings as belonging to themselves.

They feel at odds with themselves and their environment. This is why close relatives or trusted caregivers usually seek help and support, as they have developed their own psychological problems as a result of the difficult situations with the person affected. Since a personality disorder usually exists for years before those affected seek support, therapy also takes a longer period of time. Although those affected are usually unmotivated at the start of therapy, significant improvements can be observed as a result of therapy. They learn to deal with difficult and unpleasant feelings and thoughts and to modify or change specific behaviors. Interpersonal relationships can also be addressed and worked on. Therapy cannot change a person's personality. However, everyday situations and stressful conflicts can be better managed using certain learned techniques. This enables the person concerned to build and maintain better relationships with others.

If the origin of the developed personality disorder lies in childhood, depth psychology-based therapy can be beneficial. The focus of the therapy is on analyzing and working through traumatic and difficult relationships that were experienced in childhood. Cognitive-behavioral therapy programs, on the other hand, focus on social skills training. Using role-playing games or group therapy, those affected learn what behavior is appropriate in certain situations. Both cognitive-behavioral therapy and depth psychology-based methods are moderately to highly effective.

Nevertheless, the treatment of dissocial personality disorder is particularly difficult, as those affected are unable to build a trusting relationship with the therapist due to a lack of emotional warmth and empathy. The inner desire for power and violence cannot be extinguished, even in therapy. However, those affected can learn to control their urges better if they allow it.

DO YOU RECOGNIZE YOURSELF IN THE DESCRIPTIONS?

If you feel that many of these characteristics also apply to you after reading the description of the disorders, you should seek support. A diagnostic consultation with a psycho therapist will provide clarity. As a rule, these are also covered by health insurance. You do not have to be ashamed of your suspicions and behavior, nor do you have to tell your employer or anyone else about them. A psychotherapist is also subject to medical confidentiality, which means that none of your conversation with them will leave the room. A therapist is only required to act if you pose a danger to yourself or others.

However, if you don't have the confidence to see a therapist straight away, confide in someone you trust. It can usually help to talk to a trusted person and face your therapy-related fears. There are also many different offers of help on the internet. You may also find it easier to talk to like-minded people. In addition to numerous internet forums, group therapy can also be considered. A mental illness is nothing to be ashamed of. Especially when you consider that around one in four people have a mental illness.

Recognize dark techniques of psychology

You now know all about the dark triad of personality and the two dark personality disorders. You know that dark personalities achieve their own goals primarily through manipulation, lies and exploitative behavior. But once you have recognized a dark personality, how do you succeed in exposing their manipulative tricks and lies? This chapter will give you the answer to this question. You will learn how to expose lies and manipulation and how to use persuasion tactics yourself. In most cases, this is not that easy and requires a bit of practice and confidence in your own abilities.

EXPOSING LIES

Nobody likes to be lied to and manipulated. But sometimes it's not so easy to catch someone in a lie. People with dark personality traits in particular usually have years of experience in deception and manipulation. It is therefore very difficult to see through their true intentions. They don't get nervous as easily as other people when they lie.

Nevertheless, you can also learn what behavior you should pay attention to in order to expose a lie to your counterpart. Someone who has nothing to hide will normally give you a simple and short answer. For example, an innocent person is more likely to answer the question of whether you have stolen something with a clear "no". A guilty person who wants to conceal their crime will usually try to convince the other person of their innocence using various techniques and tactics.

Liars often begin their answer to a question by repeating it. This gives them time to think about how they can credibly embellish their lie. You can assume

that if you delay answering for 5 seconds, your counterpart is lying to you. That's how long the brain needs
to come up with a lie. Liars have the same ulterior motive when they repeat answers and questions during
the course of a conversation. The repetition is also intended to emphasize and clarify what has been said.
Liars also often refer to previous lies in such a conversation. They then refer to an earlier answer such as: "I
already told you last week that I didn't steal the glas-
ses." From his point of view, he is merely repeating a
previous lie by referring to it and is therefore not de-
ceiving his counterpart again. Another tactic that al-
lows you to recognize relatively quickly whether the
other person is lying to you is distraction. If the other
person tries to answer a simple question in a very long-
winded and rambling way, you can be sure that they
are trying to cover up what they have actually done.
This will prevent them from making a clear statement
about your question.

In most cases, facial expressions and gestures can
also tell you whether the other person is lying to you.
As people with a dark personality usually have a lot of
experience in lying and manipulation, it is particularly
difficult to tell from their facial features whether they
are lying or not. They have usually learned to control

their facial expressions and gestures over the years. With the help of the following signs, you may still be able to unmask a master of lies and deception:

1. **Frequent blinking**. However, you should know how often a person blinks in normal conversations in order to be able to draw a comparison.

2. **Reddened cheeks**. Blushing can hardly be suppressed, which is why it is a good indication to expose a lie.

3. **excessive movement**. You should be alert to sudden restlessness and movement after asking a question. It could go hand in hand with the emerging nervousness of telling a lie.

4. **your counterpart starts tidying up**. Other, sometimes actually unimportant activities are carried out during the conversation. Possibly out of nervousness or to distract.

5. **wide open eyes**. Wide open eyes indicate surprise, fear and panic. The other person usually needs a short time to think about their answer.

6. **sweating, trembling or frequent swallowing.** Observable physical reactions usually accompany lying.

7. **the distance is increased.** People who feel they have been caught lying usually unconsciously start to increase the distance between themselves and the other person.

8. **interlocked posture.** Many people unconsciously adopt a defensive posture when lying. They cross their arms or turn their body away from the other person.

9. **gestures and facial expressions** do not match what is said. The conversation partner often nods, although they clearly say "No".

10. **facial expressions do not match.** Eyes and mouth do not say the same thing. Laughter is usually the best way to tell whether the person opposite is serious or lying. If the eyes are not laughing, you can assume that the other person is trying to deceive you.

11 **Too many details.** To appear more credible, they embellish their lie with lots of small, mostly

unnecessary information.

However, in addition to these signs, you can also use body language and posture to recognize whether the other person would prefer to escape the situation. A good indication of this is the position of their feet. Anyone who wants to escape from a conversation usually turns their toes towards the door or away from the other person. The unconscious turning of the body towards the door can also be a sign of the need to escape. Constantly looking towards the door could also be an indication of a lie. In addition to the instinct to flee, hiding your hands under the table or in your trouser pockets can also be a sign that the other person is trying to hide something. Crossing your feet and then pulling them back under the chair also seems to be trying to hide something from you. If a person is afraid of being caught in a lie, they will quickly turn away when they make eye contact, as they are afraid that their eyes might give them away.

However, you must always bear in mind that such signs can always be due to the specific circumstances of a situation. If the other person has just finished work, it is not an indication of deception if they start tidying up their workplace before they go home. You should also have known the person you suspect of lying for some time. This is because only if they show behavior that deviates from their everyday behavior is this also an indication of a lie. For example, a person may generally be very restless and move around a lot or be anxious, so they would generally be more likely to turn towards the door. You need to observe your counterpart in everyday situations and know their behavior in order to uncover their behavior when telling lies and deceptions.

RECOGNIZE TECHNIQUES OF MANIPULATION

The term manipulation usually describes the targeted exertion of influence on the thoughts and behavior of other people. The influence is exerted covertly and is therefore often viewed negatively. People with dark personality traits in particular manipulate others for selfish and self-serving motives.

As their own goals are paramount and they accept that other people will be hurt in the process, the manipulation techniques used often lead to a negative outcome for the person being manipulated. Perhaps you too have been taken in by a manipulator? Or you want to protect yourself by finding out about the methods used by cunning manipulators? If so, this chapter will give you the opportunity to learn about manipulation techniques and strategies and how to protect yourself against them.

The easiest and probably best way to protect yourself from a manipulator is to listen to your own gut feeling. Does a situation seem strange to you? Do you find it difficult to trust a person? Then it's better to keep your distance. Many manipulation techniques work by making you feel guilty or unsettling you in other ways. However, if you appear confident and assured, it will be difficult for a manipulator to unsettle you and convince you of their ideas. Your first step should therefore be to learn to trust yourself and be at peace with yourself.

But sometimes even the most self-confident person finds it difficult to see through a manipulator and trust their gut feeling. Manipulators use clever strategies to achieve their desired goal. It can therefore be beneficial to know the 10 most commonly used manipulation strategies in order to see through a manipulator and their intentions from the outset.

1. The principle of reciprocity

The principle of reciprocity is firmly anchored in the human core. If someone does us a favor, we have the feeling that we also have to do them a favor. A manipulator can make excellent use of this principle.

He does you a small favor and takes advantage of your guilty conscience to ask you for an even bigger favor. You will find it difficult to refuse this request from him because you feel you owe him something. A simple example of this can be found in a restaurant. If the waiter puts a sweet next to the bill, the tip is usually higher.

2. Foot-in-the-door principle

With this principle, the manipulator will also ask you for a small favor. This can apparently steer you quite harmlessly in one direction and serves as a door opener. You will then do him a bigger favor much more easily, as we humans tend to be consistent. You will find it difficult to get out. For example, if he asks you to look at a presentation for an important meeting a few days beforehand, you are more likely to say yes if he then asks you if you could give the presentation with him. The important thing here is to listen to your gut feeling, take a moment and think carefully about whether you really want to do this.

3. Scarcity

A manipulator can skillfully put you under pressure by claiming that something is limited or scarce. In the case of decisions, for example, by limiting the time or number of places. You will intuitively say "yes" more quickly than without this pressure.

The principle is of course often used in advertising, where limited editions are offered. Listen to your own needs, don't let yourself be put under pressure and don't feel guilty about saying "no".

4. Playing with fear

Just as you can use limitations to exert pressure, you can also use fear to create pressure. If your counterpart tries to trigger a panicked and anxious feeling in you with sentences such as: "Tomorrow may already be too late" or "Could you really forgive yourself if you don't do anything now?", they will probably be aiming to elicit a decision from you under time pressure and fear. Again, take your time to think things through and don't make any hasty decisions.

5. The likeable friend

This technique is based on the psychological principle that we find it difficult to refuse a wish from a person who is very similar and likeable to ourselves.

A manipulator exploits this by pretending to have similar interests to you and also mirroring your body language. This will make it easier for them to convince you to do them a favor. Again, just knowing about this principle will make you question his hobbies and interests critically. If you find a situation strange or uncomfortable, see if the other person mirrors your posture and body signals. A typical example of this is a salesperson who casually mentions that they have the same hobbies as the potential buyer.

6. The authority principle

Manipulators use and acquire titles to appear credible and trustworthy. People are less likely to question his judgment because he is an expert. They try to use their title or expert status to make false arguments sound credible.

Check his statements if something seems strange to you, or ask about his CV and try to expose his lies. Another example of exploiting the authority principle is when the manipulator tries to get ahead of your boss by claiming: "The boss said ...". Here, too, you should address your boss personally if the request is atypical. In the best case scenario, the manipulation attempt can then be unmasked immediately.

7. Selective information transfer

A relatively frequently used manipulation technique is to omit or emphasize certain information. If you therefore have the feeling that something is being withheld from you, follow up on this. Try as far as possible to obtain your own information and also see what interests your counterpart represents. A possible conflict of interest could be the reason for omitting relevant information.

8. Overinformation

In contrast to omitting information, this manipulation strategy consists of presenting an oversupply of information.

Your counterpart tries to overwhelm you with mostly unimportant information for so long that you end up not knowing what the conversation is actually about. If you come home confused from a conversation with too much information, you should ask yourself once again exactly what the aim of the conversation was supposed to be.

9. Followership

We humans have the need to join groups. What many others do will be right. But that's where things can get dangerous. If you always just follow along and don't question what others are doing, you can quickly be manipulated. Social peer pressure in particular should be avoided here.

10. Emotional blackmail

The manipulator usually tries to blackmail you with feelings using this tactic. The focus is on strongly negative and stressful feelings. People usually agree to the demands in order to avoid conflict. This strategy is often used in partnerships in particular, as there is an emotional dependency here. You are often made to feel guilty, reproached and threatened.

This can lead to you developing depression as a result of your feelings of guilt. Therefore, pay close attention to your partner's accusations and threats such as: "If you really loved me, you wouldn't do something like this", "I've given up so much because of you ..." or "I don't know if I can still be with you if you do something like this." You shouldn't let these remarks get to you, but discuss these accusations with your partner as equals and confront them.

Not every manipulation has a malicious intention. Sometimes, for example, the omission of information may not have had a consciously malicious motive. Manipulation strategies are often used in negotiations to achieve a desired result. However, if manipulation techniques go hand in hand with hurting and taking advantage of other people in order to achieve one's own goals, urgent action should be taken.

APPLY PSYCHOLOGY TECHNI-QUES

After you have learned how to recognize and expose manipulation and lies, in this chapter you will learn how you can convince your counterpart of your arguments in negotiation or persuasion discussions. You will now learn how to use psychological techniques to achieve your goal. However, make sure you always remain friendly and objective.

Learn negotiation and persuasion tactics

Persuasive tactics can be found everywhere in everyday life. People usually use persuasion tactics when they want to achieve a certain goal and want to get others on board to help them achieve it. Of course, you could also make decisions on your own.

But we humans are creatures that strive for socially acceptable solutions. For example, you are more likely to try to persuade your partner to buy a new TV via than to go it alone. All you need for this kind of persuasion are tactics and convincing arguments. According to psychologist Noah Goldstein, the effectiveness of the conscious use of persuasion strategies has been scientifically proven. It can also be useful to use tactics and strategies to achieve your own goals in negotiation discussions. Especially if you want to negotiate successfully, you will not be able to avoid these techniques. In addition to a confident appearance, the following 10 strategies can help you to convince others of your arguments. Conversely, you can also use the techniques presented to recognize when someone is trying to convince you strategically.

1. Control feelings

The more neutral you appear during a negotiation, the better you can convince your counterpart. Open and honest answers and a sense of humor will also make you appear more convincing.

If, on the other hand, you are negotiating with a manipulator or a person with dark personality traits, you should think carefully beforehand about how openly and honestly you present your arguments, because your counterpart will continue to try to manipulate you.

2. Make the first offer.

Scientific studies show that the first offer during a conversation or even a negotiation is used as a benchmark for subsequent arguments and offers. You can take advantage of this knowledge by arguing first and setting the benchmark in this way. Psychologists refer to this as the anchor effect.

3. Give compliments.

People with and without dark personality traits also love to receive compliments and praise in persuasive conversations. You can make particularly good use of compliments before a persuasive conversation.

For example, if you expect a person to be very understanding of a situation, you can start the day before by describing your conversation partner as very understanding. The likelihood that your conversation partner will be understanding of your situation the next day increases significantly.

4. Small steps.

Don't open the door straight away. If you want to convince your counterpart to make a big change, start with small steps first. Most people don't like change, so take away their fear by gradually introducing them to your goal. Use the "foot in the door principle" described above by asking for a small favor first and then the bigger one later.

5. Make comparisons.

Since we humans are herd animals, we tend to be convinced by the masses. Take advantage of this weakness by making comparisons such as: "My friend has also bought a new television and is very happy with it." Comparisons increase the likelihood of convincing your counterpart.

6. few alternatives.

Always point out alternatives in negotiation discussions. People are afraid of being unable to act and therefore need alternative courses of action when criticized. You must present ways out of the situation.

However, make sure that you present as few concrete alternatives as possible. Otherwise, the other person will feel overwhelmed and will need considerably more time to make a decision. Studies have shown that if people are offered too many options, they will postpone or completely avoid choosing the right option.

7. tactical silence.

Hardly anyone can stand silence in conversations or negotiations. You can use this to your advantage. Make your demand and remain silent. Look the other person in the eye and wait. Most people find this very uncomfortable and will try to break the silence. But remain firm. Do not respond to resistance, but repeat your demand. Your counterpart will try to break your silence again with justifications. As time goes on, they will use weaker and weaker arguments to break the silence. All you have to do is wait and refute their weak arguments in the end.

8. create feelings of guilt.

Just as skillful manipulators try to create feelings of guilt in others in order to get their way, you can also use this technique. For example, try to take your counterpart's demands to extremes in negotiations.

Feel free to exaggerate and make him feel guilty about his own demands. For example, as a manager you could say: "If everyone took as much vacation as you do, there would be no one left for our customers and we could close the store."

9. do not present all strong arguments immediately.

Make sure that you start your negotiation with a strong argument. Save up an equally strong argument until you realize that the other party is getting tired. If you then present another strong argument, your counterpart will give in more quickly and make concessions to you.

10. pay attention to the end.

Try to stay focused until the end of the negotiation. Even after reaching an agreement, use the last few minutes of the meeting to make your demands. Question everything again at the end and add another demand. Your negotiating partner will be tired and listless and will therefore be too quick to give in to your new demand.

With the help of the persuasion and negotiation tactics presented above, it is unlikely that anyone will refuse you anything so quickly. However, be careful not to be mean or spiteful to the person you are talking to at . Use the conversation techniques and stick to your moral principles and boundaries. The techniques can be used individually during the conversation. However, you should pay attention to what the primary goal of your conversation is.

Do you want to convince your partner to change the color of the walls in your bedroom or do you want to negotiate with your boss for more money? Different objectives require different approaches. Make sure you are sufficiently prepared for a negotiation and therefore avoid negotiating at short notice.

This way, you won't be taken by surprise by your counterpart and can make confident decisions. As a general rule, always maintain eye contact during a conversation, appear confident and be aware of the extent of your actions. For example, if you make someone feel guilty in order to achieve your goal, you should be aware beforehand that you can reconcile this with your personal moral standards. Always appear friendly and sympathetic and don't be afraid to ask specific questions if something is unclear. Use your language in a targeted manner, as it usually accounts for a large part of your success.

WHAT YOU HAVE NOW LEARNED

I hope you have found what you were looking for in this guide and that it has met your expectations. You have learned what constitutes a dark personality and how to recognize it. You can now see through and expose lies and manipulation techniques. You know how you should approach a person with dark character traits and what you should avoid in social interactions. If possible, keep your distance and don't get involved in the games. Because, although you now have extensive knowledge, dark personalities are masters of deception and will find a way to harm you.

If someone around you shows signs of a personality disorder, don't hesitate to approach them gently and look for possible relief together. However, don't tie a brick to your leg. It is usually difficult to help people with a personality disorder without professional help. Take care of yourself and your health and learn to say "no" sometimes. You too can use the persuasion and negotiation techniques presented here to hold successful discussions and achieve your goals. Of course, this always depends on the circumstances of the situation.

Nevertheless, you can try to use one or two strategies in your next conversation to get one step closer to the desired result.